Y0-EEA-800

R01374 92530

WORLD CELEBRATIONS AND CEREMONIES

Coming of Age

by

Lisa Sita

WORLD CELEBRATIONS AND CEREMONIES

BLACKBIRCH PRESS, INC.

WOODBRIDGE, CONNECTICUT

Published by Blackbirch Press, Inc.
260 Amity Road
Woodbridge, CT 06525

©1999 by Blackbirch Press, Inc.
First Edition

e-mail: staff@blackbirch.com
Web site: www.blackbirch.com

Printed in the United States

10 9 8 7 6 5 4 3 2 1

Photo Credits
Cover photo: Courtesy of the United Nations; pages
3 and 11: ©Steve Vidler/Leo de Wys Inc.; pages 4 and
5: ©Victor Englebert; page 7: ©Bob Krist; page 8:
©Courtesy of Air-India Library; page 9: ©Elliott Smith/
International Stock; page 13: ©Paul J. Buklarewicz;
pages 14–15: ©D. Donne Bryant/DDB Stock Photo;
page 17: ©Jason Lauré; page 19: ©D. Westerman/
International Stock; page 21: ©Jeffrey Aaronson/
Network Aspen; page 22: ©Stephen Trimble.

**Library of Congress
Cataloging-in-Publication Data**
Sita, Lisa.
Coming of age/ by Lisa Sita.
        p.   cm. —(World celebrations and ceremonies)
        Includes bibliographical references and index.
        Summary: Describes initiation rites and coming of
age ceremonies of various cultural groups from around
the world including the Yanomami, Hindu, Jewish,
Puerto Rican, and Apache Indians.
        ISBN 1-56711-276-5 (lib. bdg.)
        1. Puberty rites—Juvenile literature. 1. Initiation
rites—Juvenile literature. 1. Rites and ceremonies—
Juvenile literature. [1. Initiation rites. 2. Rites and
ceremonies.] I. Title. II. Series.
GN483.3.S57   1999
658.4'012—dc21   98-13506
                                                  CIP
                                                  AC

❂ CONTENTS ❂

⊚ INTRODUCTION ⊚

Coming of age is a special time in a person's life. When a child comes of age, it means that he or she has taken an important step toward growing up. A young adult, with new rights, must now behave in a responsible way. In most places around the world, there is a ceremony to honor this important change in a young person's life. It is often a time for celebrating with family and friends. At a Mexican girl's *Quince Años* (KEEN-say AN-yos), people have a party that lasts for two days. Some coming-of-age ceremonies are serious religious events, such as a child's First Holy Communion in Puerto Rico. Some important steps in growing up and coming of age are made very quietly. It may be the day an English child leaves for boarding school. Or it may be the week a Yanomami boy from Brazil goes hunting with the men in his community. No matter how it is celebrated, a coming-of-age event brings a child closer to becoming a man or woman.

3

BRAZIL

In some places, children learn adult skills by playing or by helping adults. Yanomami children help grown-ups cook wild foods. They live in the Amazon rain forest of Brazil, far from large cities, such as São Paulo. Yanomami boys play at hunting. They catch small animals, such as lizards and frogs. When a Yanomami boy is older, he goes on a real hunt. He joins the men and hunts for his family. He also hunts for the community—the people who live in the same area.

ⓢ · ⓢ · ⓢ · ⓢ · ⓢ · ⓢ · ⓢ · ⓢ · ⓢ · ⓢ · ⓢ

Brazil has the largest rain forest in the world. It is a warm place that gets a lot of rain. Many different kinds of plants grow there. Some of them are used to make medicine.

ⓢ · ⓢ · ⓢ · ⓢ · ⓢ · ⓢ · ⓢ · ⓢ · ⓢ · ⓢ · ⓢ

Young girls copy adult women by cooking small meals.

When a boy is allowed to hunt with men, that is a sign that the community thinks he has come of age. Another sign is when people stop using his name in public. The Yanomami think it is impolite to say a man's name in front of other people. Instead, they use a family title, like "brother" or "nephew." When a boy begins to feel he is growing up, he will get angry if he is not shown this sign of respect.

A young boy learns to be a man by playing at hunting.

A Yanomami girl comes of age when she reaches puberty. That is when her body begins to look like a woman's body. When that happens, she is separated from everyone else in her house. She stays behind a screen of leaves, where she is cared for and fed by her relatives for about a week. Afterward, she can marry.

Key for All Country Maps

★ *Capital city* ■ *Major city*

ENGLAND

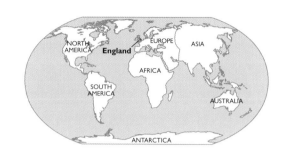

In many communities, a child takes a number of important steps as she or he grows up. Each step teaches a child new responsibilities. These events are not always celebrated with ceremonies, but they are important because they bring the child closer to being an adult.

In England, some children take such a step by leaving home to live in a boarding school. Students who go to boarding school come from large cities, such as London, and small towns in the countryside. Boarding schools are private schools. This means that the students' parents pay for their education.

Some children go to a type of boarding school called a "preparatory school." They go there from the ages of 7 to 13.

⦿ · ⦿ · ⦿ · ⦿ · ⦿ · ⦿ · ⦿ · ⦿ · ⦿ · ⦿ · ⦿

England is part of an island called Great Britain. The island also includes Scotland and Wales. Between Great Britain and the main part of Europe is a narrow body of water called the English Channel.

⦿ · ⦿ · ⦿ · ⦿ · ⦿ · ⦿ · ⦿ · ⦿ · ⦿ · ⦿ · ⦿

Some English children go away to boarding school when they are seven years old.

Afterward, they go on to the next level of education, known as "public school." These public schools may also be boarding schools, where students can live. Before graduating from school, English children must take tests. They need good scores to get accepted to universities.

For some English children, going away to boarding school is one step on the way to becoming an adult. By leaving their families and living at school, these students learn how to take care of themselves. Their new responsibilities help them grow into successful adults.

INDIA

After taking part in his Upanayanam, *a Hindu boy is treated like a man.*

In India, boys who worship in the Hindu faith have a special way to come of age. They take part in the ceremony called *Upanayanam* (oo-pa-NA-YA-nam). At this ritual, a boy between 8 and 12 years of age becomes a full member of his religious community. Only boys belonging to the top castes in India take part in this ceremony. (Hindus believe that people are born into certain social positions, called "castes.")

The day for the *Upanayanam* is chosen by an astrologer. That is a person who studies the motion of stars and planets. Many people believe that stars and planets can affect events on Earth. The astrologer studies where the planets and stars will be on a certain day. Then he or she can choose a lucky day for the event.

During the *Upanayanam*, a boy has a special white cotton thread placed around him. This thread is tied into a loop. First it must be blessed by a Hindu priest.

India is in southern Asia. This land has a very long history. People have been living in this part of the world for more than 5,000 years.

The priest prays over the thread in front of a holy fire. The fire represents energy and cleanliness. Then the priest places the looped thread over the boy's left shoulder and under his right arm. After he has received the thread, the boy learns a prayer called the *Gayatri Mantra* (GA-ya-tree MAN-tra). It can be heard only by those who have also gone through an *Upanayanam*.

By receiving this thread, a boy shows that he is starting a new life. He is now treated like an adult member of his Hindu community.

This Hindu temple is in eastern India.

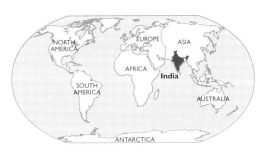

ISRAEL

At the age of 13, Jewish boys in Israel—and throughout the world—celebrate their *Bar Mitzvah* (bar mits-VAH). This important ceremony marks when a boy becomes an adult in the Jewish community.

Bar Mitzvah is Hebrew for "son of the commandments." When a boy becomes *Bar Mitzvah*, he is responsible for obeying the commandments, or laws, of the Jewish people. He also receives certain privileges. For example, he can be counted as part of a *minyan* (min-YAN). That is a group of at least ten men who gather to pray.

Before his *Bar Mitzvah*, a boy studies Jewish laws and the Hebrew language. On the day of his *Bar Mitzvah*, he reads from the *Torah* (toe-RAH). It is a copy of the Bible that is written in Hebrew on a long roll of animal skin.

A *Bar Mitzvah* usually happens in a synagogue, where Jewish people pray. It is often led by a rabbi, who is a religious leader. Sometimes the ceremony is held at the Western Wall in Jerusalem.

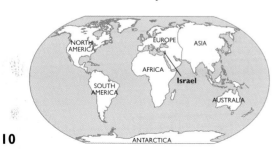

This wall was once part of an ancient Jewish temple, and it is very holy.

Bar Mitzvahs were once only for boys. But, in recent times, girls have also enjoyed this ceremony. Girls become *Bat Mitzvah* (bot mits-VAH), which means "daughters of the commandments," at the age of 12.

An Israeli boy celebrates his Bar Mitzvah *with his family at the Western Wall.*

JAPAN

In Japan, there is a special ceremony for young men and women who have reached their twentieth birthdays. It is observed in cities such as Tokyo and in small communities around the island. It is called the Coming-of-Age Ceremony, and it takes place on January 15 each year. On that day, young men and women who have reached their twentieth birthday take part in special events.

Each Japanese community holds a Coming-of-Age Ceremony for its young people. Everyone gets dressed up and has his or her picture taken by a photographer. Young women wear a traditional Japanese kimono. A kimono is a robe-like dress or jacket that is wrapped around the body and tied with a wide sash. Some kimonos are made of silk. They are very expensive and are often handed down from mother to daughter. Many have colorful designs.

The island nation of Japan is part of the continent of Asia. Japan is one of the most important centers for business in the world.

At her Coming-of-Age Ceremony, a 20-year-old woman usually wears a kimono that has been in her family for a long time. Although young men may also wear kimonos, most of them wear suits and ties.

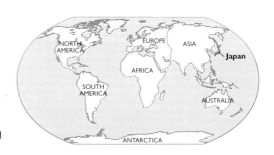

The event takes place in a town hall or other public building. Important members of the community, such as the mayor, make speeches. They tell the young people that now, as adults, they must be good citizens. The young people answer by reading poems or short pieces of writing about their new rights and responsibilities. According to Japanese law, 20-year-olds are adults. They may vote in elections and they are officially responsible for their behavior.

A young woman and a young man celebrate their Coming-of-Age Ceremony with a photograph.

MEXICO

In Mexico, a girl celebrates her coming of age on her fifteenth birthday. This special birthday is called her *Quince Años* (KEEN-say AN-yos). In Spanish this means "15 years." A *Quince Años* celebration is common in small villages, and in big cities such as Mexico City. The celebration is a long and happy one.

On this day, dressed in a long gown, a Mexican girl is the center of attention. In the morning, the girl's friends and relatives arrive with presents for her. Musicians play the Mexican birthday song, *Las Mañanitas* (las man-ya-NEE-tas). Then everyone eats breakfast and goes to church for a special birthday mass. A mass is a Roman Catholic religious service.

After the mass, there is a big party. Sometimes it's at the girl's home. There are delicious foods like rice and chicken *mole* (MO-lay). *Mole* is a kind of sauce that can be made with many ingredients, including chocolate and spices.

Mexico is part of the continent of North America. Many tourists from all over the world vacation at Mexico's beaches along the Pacific Ocean.

Flowers and music are part of the celebration for a girl's Quince Años.

There is also a birthday cake. Everyone dances, including the girl of honor and her father. As her *Quince Años* ends, a Mexican girl is ready to date boys.

UNITED STATES

Monterrey

MEXICO

Guadalajara

Mexico City

Pacific Ocean

Gulf of Mexico

BELIZE

GUATEMALA

N W E S

NIGERIA

The Hausa are a Muslim people who live in northern Nigeria, far from the big city of Lagos. Muslim people follow a religion called Islam. A Hausa girl becomes a woman when she gets married. So her

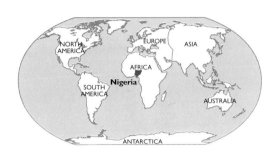

wedding is also her coming-of-age ceremony. Many Hausa girls get married in their late teens. But boys do not usually get married until they are in their early twenties. That is when they can work and support a wife and children.

A Hausa wedding ceremony goes on for about a week. Because

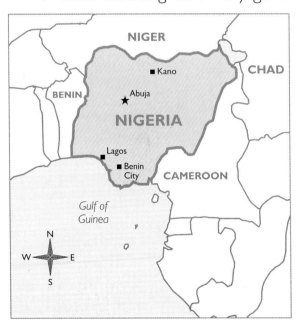

the wedding is also a coming-of-age ceremony, the bride and groom celebrate separately with their friends and families. Sometimes the celebrations are in two different towns. During the week of the wedding, gifts are exchanged between the families of the bride and groom. Afterward, the bride leaves her parents' home and goes to live with her husband.

Because they are Muslim, the Hausa practice the custom of *purdah* (PURR-dah). *Purdah* means that a married woman must always stay inside her husband's home. That is where she will be protected and supported by him. She can leave the house only for very special events. Men are not allowed to enter a house where another man's wife is staying. Only children and old women may move freely between the worlds of men and women. When a Hausa girl marries and becomes an adult, she must get used to this great change in her life.

Hausa girls come of age when they get married.

Nigeria is on the continent of Africa. About 250 different groups of people live in Nigeria, and almost 250 languages are spoken there.

PUERTO RICO

Puerto Rico is an island in the Caribbean Sea. Many Puerto Ricans live in cities along the coast, such as the capital city of San Juan.

🌀 · 🌀 · 🌀 · 🌀 · 🌀 · 🌀 · 🌀 · 🌀 · 🌀 · 🌀 · 🌀

In Puerto Rico, most people belong to the Catholic religion. From the capital city of San Juan to the small towns, Catholic children look forward to their First Holy Communion. This is the first step in becoming a grown-up member of their religious community.

Communion is part of a Catholic religious service called "mass." During mass, a priest makes a blessing over a wafer (a thin cracker) which is called the "host." He also blesses a cup of wine mixed with water. Catholics believe that when the wafer and the wine are blessed, they become the body and blood of Jesus Christ. During mass, a priest offers the host to everyone in church except young children. By eating the host, a person makes a connection, or a "communion," with God. (Catholics also believe that Jesus Christ is the Son of God.)

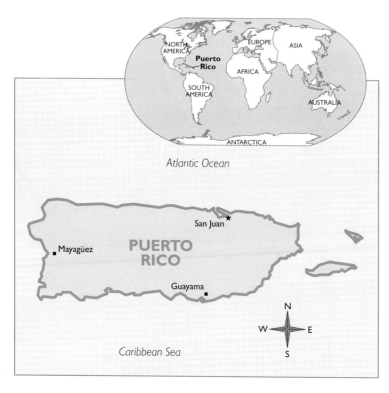

Atlantic Ocean

Caribbean Sea

When children make their First Holy Communion, it is the first time they take the host. They can now participate completely at every mass by taking the host, just as adults do.

First Holy Communion happens when a child is about eight years old. Four or five years later, Catholic children in Puerto Rico and other countries take part in another ceremony called Confirmation. At Confirmation, children promise to live by the teachings of the Catholic Church. At their Confirmation, they show that they are ready to be responsible for all their actions. They are now treated as adult members of the church.

A First Communion is a step in becoming a grown-up member of the Catholic community.

RUSSIA

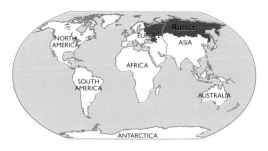

Sometimes children begin taking steps toward adulthood on their own, when they feel ready. In the Russian Orthodox religion, a child does not celebrate his or her coming of age with a large ceremony. But, children do show that they are growing up in a religious way—when they first do Confession.

Russia is the largest country in the world. Most people live in cities in the west and south. Siberia, in the northern part of the country, is always cold.

The Russian Orthodox faith is a Christian religion. This means that its teachings are based on the life and words of Jesus Christ. The church teaches its members the right way to behave. When someone does something wrong, he or she must confess. Confession allows a person to admit a mistake.

If the person is sorry, Russian Orthodox people believe he or she may ask God for forgiveness and receive it.

A Russian Orthodox child may be as young as six or seven at the time of a First Confession. The child goes to a church in a large city, such as Moscow, or in a small town. There the child tells his or her sins, or mistakes, to a priest. The priest acts in the

A young Russian woman lights a candle in a Russian Orthodox church.

place of God. He can forgive the child. By going to their First Confession, Russian Orthodox children show that they are beginning to take responsibility for their behavior.

UNITED STATES

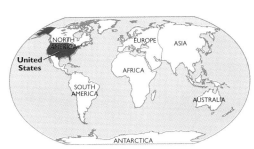

The Apache people live in the southwestern United States. The region includes states such as New Mexico, Utah, and Arizona. Like other Americans, the Apache celebrate coming-of-age ceremonies such as high school and college graduations. But the Apache also have a special ceremony to honor a girl's coming of age.

A girl is painted with clay to give her the "power of the earth."

For the Apache, a girl's coming of age begins with puberty. A girl's puberty ceremony lasts four days. It is led by a religious person called a "medicine man." During the ceremony, the girl is supposed to take the place of "White Painted Woman."

The Apache believe that she is an important holy woman who first brought the puberty ritual to them. Like White Painted Woman, the girl must behave properly and set a good example. She is helped by an older woman who has been chosen as her godmother.

Throughout the ceremony, the girl sits in a shelter made of saplings, or young trees. Inside the shelter is a buckskin—a strong but soft material made out of the skin of a deer. The girl dances on the buckskin during the day. At night, large fires are lit, and everyone dances. There is a special dance given by men who are dressed to look like *gan* (gahn). According to the Apache, *gan* are spirits who live in the mountains. The *gan* dancers wear body paint and tall headdresses, which are special head coverings. The *gan* help to bring blessings and good fortune.

If the ceremony is done correctly, the girl will have a good life and be a responsible adult.

The United States has two neighbors on its borders. To the north is Canada, and to the south is Mexico.

Glossary

caste According to the Hindu religion, a person's social position.

ceremony Actions, words, or music that mark a special occasion.

community People who are connected to each other in some way.

gan According to the Apache, spirits who live in the mountains.

host In the Catholic religion, the wafer that is believed to become the body of Christ.

kimono A type of robe that Japanese people wear on special occasions.

minyan A group of at least ten Jewish men who gather to pray.

mole A sauce that can be made with many ingredients, including chocolate and spices.

privileges Special treatment and rights.

puberty The time when a person's body starts to become like an adult's.

purdah The practice among Muslim women of staying in their homes.

Further Reading

Hermes, Jules. *The Children of India* (The World's Children series). Minneapolis: Carolrhoda Books, Inc., 1993.

Kimmel, Eric A. *Bar Mitzvah: A Jewish Boy's Coming of Age.* New York: Viking Children's Books, 1996.

Schomp, Virginia. *Russia: New Freedoms, New Challenges* (Exploring Cultures of the World series). Tarrytown, NY: Marshall Cavendish, 1996.

Schwartz, David M. *Yanomami, People of the Amazon.* New York: Lothrop, Lee & Shepard Books, 1995.

Sita, Lisa. *The Rattle and the Drum: Native American Rituals and Celebrations.* Brookfield, CT: Millbrook Press, 1994.

Tourism Web Sites

Brazil: http://www.brazilinfo.com

England: http://www.visitbritain.com

India: http://www.tourindia.com

Israel: http://www.goisrael.com

Japan: http://www.jnto.go.jp

Mexico: http://www.mexico-travel.com

Nigeria: http://www.sas.upenn.edu/African_Studies/Country_Specific/Nigeria.htm

Puerto Rico: http://www.Welcome.toPuertoRico.org

Russia: http://www.tours.ru

United States: http://www.united-states.com

Index